A Pocket Full Of Maybe

Poetic Musings on Being

Kayla Goodman

BookLeaf Publishing
India | USA | UK

Made with ❤ on the BookLeaf Publishing Platform
www.bookleafpub.in
www.bookleafpub.com

Dedication

To my teachers —
The ones who shaped and formed me.
Thank you for seeing potential when I could not yet see it myself.
Thank you for lighting paths of curiosity, courage, and compassion.
Your patience, wisdom, and belief have shaped not just my mind, but my life.
This book is a small reflection of the many lessons you planted in me.
I carry your influence with gratitude and hope.

Preface

This collection was never meant to be neat or polished.
It grew out of scattered thoughts, quiet moments, and
the kind of questions that don't always have answers.
Each poem is a snapshot of feeling — sometimes messy,
sometimes clear — stitched together by a hope to
understand, to remember, to become.
These words are pieces of my journey, offered with the
hope that they might find a home somewhere in yours
too.
Thank you for stepping into these pages with me.
I hope you find something here that speaks to where
you've been, where you are, or where you're going.

Acknowledgements

This book would not exist without the many people who shaped me, encouraged me, and believed in my voice.

To my teachers — thank you for inspiring curiosity and resilience. You taught me that words have weight and that stories matter.

To my friends and family — thank you for listening when the words got stuck, for celebrating small milestones, and for reminding me why I write.

To every quiet moment, every difficult season, every unexpected joy — thank you for giving me something to say.

And finally, to the reader — thank you for opening these pages. May you find a piece of yourself here, and may these words meet you kindly.

Just Here

Is it enough
just here
showing up
or must I
do more?
life feels
like a chore
but instead
of going away
I choose to
stay.
so I think
it is enough
to just
be here
today.

Waves of Brilliance

There is a fire
burning in my bones
an aliveness
trying to escape me

How can I
learn to see
more of the
beauty around me

The sky is
illuminated with
brilliance of the waves
of the colors of the wind

May I encounter
the breeze of grace
that leaves its trace
in every corner of creation

Learning to Fly

How do I soar
On these wings which have been told
They are not suited for
Flying

Because of the fear
Of me flying higher
Then the boundaries
Of the rows of trees
Meant to keep me
From exploring
How far I can
Go

They let my wings
Warp in deformity
Even amidst my cries
For help

It's nothing

They said
The pain of what
“nothing” brought me
Stabs and jabs all day.

Finding My Way

There is a fist
Pounding the ground
Dirt scattering
A methodic thump
Something rumbles
Inside me
Where do I go
From here
How do I know
Which path
To choose?
How do I
Choose me?

Creating

Create
That is my inscape
Through creation
With elation
I can format
And speak
Words beyond words
Which I could share
Stories are formed
In creating
A shaping
a molding
a reckoning.
Through the stillness
the feelings felt
bring about writing
and beauty
beyond my wildest
imagination.
If I needed to do

only one
thing forever
I would
create.

These Hands

These hands that I hold
Old and frail
Bones protruding
Skin weakening
Hold stories
Beyond comprehension

And yet the gentle
Grip of her hands in mine
Tells me a story of a heart
One reflecting the Divine

These hands
Have mended
Not only with thread
They have fed
Not only with food
They have loved
The generations of before
They have cleared

The path for more

These hands
May look old
With chipped nails
And skin folds
These hands hold
Stories of power, hope, and love
Echoing the story of His hands above

Listening Deeper

The moon never apologizes for changing,
so why do I?
The stars don't keep themselves from shining,
so why do I?
The earth does not care about how much space it takes
up,
so why do I?
Why can I not embrace
change like the moon?
Why can I not acknowledge
that I shine like the stars?
Why can I not love my space
like the earth?
Let me
change
shine
take up space

Accepting

I hope you know
how loved you are
Even by strangers
who observe from afar.

The room smiles when you enter
You relieve the tension
Never trying to be the center
You calm the commotion

My darling look
I wish you could see
That the pain you took
and made into a scene

A scene of love and
of acceptance
I only wish you could
learn to accept you too.

“Be where your feet are”

“Be where your feet are”
Yet my feet didn’t guide me here
My feet only listen
to the direct instructions from my head
and yet my feet brought me here
why do I feel dead
My heart feels empty
nowhere near full
I am being drained
moving where pulled
I want to be present
Here at this instance
Yet part of me longs
to keep starring from a distance
May I be here
make it clear
to be where
my feet are
also needs my

head and heart there
also.

Energy Magnet

Everything around me
Seemingly sucked into a funnel
to be put in me
Energy, feelings, sights and sounds
I carry them all, give them to me.

I am a collector of all sorts
Yet stories are my favorite
I am learning not to carry
these things for others.

They bog me down like
my messy floor
May I pick myself up
dusting me off. And
remember I am tough

Yet I can turn my
receiver off. I need
not carry, that which

will make me weary.
May I release so I can
walk more freely.

Tears

flowing
falling
feeling
tears.
They never
seem to dry
Why do I
cry
Every time
there is such
big emotion
due to my
devotion
to humanity.
Why when I speak
I creek in
the breaking
of my voice
Do I have
a choice?

or are
tears all
that define
me?

Her Glory

And just like that she appeared
Not like an apparition out of nowhere.
She has always been here

Often buried under the walls
she herself built so tall
to be a fortress of protection

but did I mention
over those walls behind locked doors
She has been there

waiting to be restored and reunited

to herself. She has always been here,
yet when she knew it was safe
That was when she would reappear

But the world is not safe
It never has been

So she decided to be herself instead.

To undue the constraints of her
perfectly chained story
The unfolding and undoing

THAT will be her glory

If only to tell how she felt
She fell in love with herself
Worth the discovery of who

she was always meant to be.
So yes, she appeared,
and also has always been here.

Bestfriend

I do not see
Why you chose me
to be your friend
I'll love until the end
you make me
so happy
and I feel seen.
The way the sun
sees the flower
you know not the power
you have over me
you have given
me a chance to
know and be
known. No one else
has ever given that
to me.

-bestfriend

Learning to Listen

How do I learn
the language of my heart?
How can I finally listen
to the words I've ignored
For so long I've been told
Not to listen within
When my brokenness
just wanted to heal too.

I am tired of ignoring
the voice inside
Because she has been
speaking truth and light.
Maybe one day I'll listen
before I hush her and
maybe just maybe
I'll learn to trust her

Seeking Bliss

I don't want to miss
seeing you find bliss
you've searched
to find your star
yet you were never far
from finding the key
Remember in your heart
That this is the part
of separation of old
and of new
the story continues
to unfold
keep seeking
It is out there

May I Find

May I find
joy amidst
sorrow
delight
among pain
and love
at the
sound of
hate

It Will Be Alright

May I be wild
like the ocean
or the reeds
or the wildflowers
and the trees.
May I find
love and life
May I know
it will be
alright

Winner

I won
not the game
but the time
spent with those
I love
it is all about
cherishing these
sacred moments,
as the gifts
they are.

Safety

May I love all
the rough edges
because just maybe
the sharpness
keeps me safe.

Fullness

Oh, to be full
of love
of peace
of hope
surrounded by
joy and laughter
all made possible
because of the
sorrow and tragedy
that befall your door.
My darling
you are so strong.
Relax your stance
there is no one to fight now.
Rest in the
wholeheartedness
of this home
in you.

Stretching Beyond

I am stretching
spreading my winds
for I know not yet
how far I'll go
yet I know I'll break
the limitations set
before me
I am not one
to be trapped
you will see
me fly
higher than
you thought
possible
watch me
defy all I know

www.ingramcontent.com/pod-product-compliance
Lightning Source LLC
Chambersburg PA
CBHW051749130826
49812CB00033B/1074
* 9 7 8 9 3 7 0 9 2 0 2 2 4 *